The Teacher's Lunchbox

The Teacher's Lunchbox

LEARNING TO ENJOY THE HOME SCHOOL JOURNEY

Crystal Vance

WESTBOW
PRESS
A DIVISION OF THOMAS NELSON

WestBow Press books may be ordered through booksellers or by contacting:

WestBow Press
A Division of Thomas Nelson
1663 Liberty Drive
Bloomington, IN 47403
www.westbowpress.com
1-(866) 928-1240

Because of the dynamic nature of the Internet, any web addresses or links contained in
this book may have changed since publication and may no longer be valid. The views
expressed in this work are solely those of the author and do not necessarily reflect the
views of the publisher, and the publisher hereby disclaims any responsibility for them.

Scripture taken from the Holy Bible, New International Version®. Copyright ©
1973, 1978, 1984 Biblica. Used by permission of Zondervan. All rights reserved.

Scripture quotations are from The Holy Bible, English Standard Version®
(ESV®), copyright © 2001 by Crossway, a publishing ministry of
Good News Publishers. Used by permission. All rights reserved.

Scripture quotations taken from the New American Standard Bible®,
Copyright © 1960, 1962, 1963, 1968, 1971, 1972, 1973, 1975, 1977, 1995 by
The Lockman Foundation. Used by permission." (www.Lockman.org)

Scripture taken from the New King James Version. Copyright 1979, 1980,
1982 by Thomas Nelson, inc. Used by permission. All rights reserved.

Scripture taken from the King James Version of the Bible.

Scripture quotations in this publication are taken from The Message.
Copyright © by Eugene H. Peterson 1993, 1994, 1995, 1996, 2000,
2001, 2002. Used by permission of NavPress Publishing Group.

Certain stock imagery © Thinkstock.
Any people depicted in stock imagery provided by Thinkstock are models,
and such images are being used for illustrative purposes only.

ISBN: 978-1-4497-2268-5 (sc)

Library of Congress Control Number: 2011914428

Printed in the United States of America

WestBow Press rev. date: 10/5/2011

I lovingly dedicate this book
to my first and greatest teachers,
my parents, Charlie and Betty Minor.

Because of your sacrifices to provide me
with a quality education and your love
and support through the years since,
this one is for you.

"It is good to have an end to journey toward, but it is the journey that matters, in the end."

~Ursula K. LeGuin

Contents

PART ONE: Ingredients for a healthy lunch............. 1

Introduction: *Sharing my lunch with you*........................ 3

Chapter One: Lay a firm foundation
Understanding why you home school 5

Chapter Two: Understand learning differences
Identifying your child's learning style 13

Chapter Three: Navigate the curriculum chaos
Choosing the right curriculum for your children 23

Chapter Four: Create a workable schedule
Discovering freedom in planning 31

Chapter Five: Hasten to offer praise
Motivating your children with heartfelt praise 39

Chapter Six: Begin each day anew
Accepting grace on your worst days 47

Chapter Seven: Optimize your efficiency
Getting the most out of your day 57

Chapter Eight: Exercise
Maintaining a healthy lifestyle..................................... 65

**PART TWO: "I'll trade you my apple
for your gummy worms."** 73

Special thanks to . . .

My husband, Mike, who has given his full support since day one of this journey. With so many moms who long to home school their children, but do not have the encouragement of their spouses, I do not take your support lightly. Thank you for your patience on those days when things did not go according to plan. Thank you for your efforts in building bird nests and models of the Jewish tabernacle. Thank you for the late nights spent dissecting earthworms and perch. Thank you for the weekly parent/teacher conferences (a.k.a. date nights) at Starbucks. Most of all, thank you for being a godly husband and father. God blessed me when He gave me you. I love you.

Maddy, my oldest and a natural born leader. Because you were the first child we took on this journey, we did a lot of experimenting with respect to how to do this thing right. You endured like a real trooper and made this experience so much more enjoyable. You make me very proud, not just because of your academic achievements, but because of who you are as a person. My fondest memories of this journey with you are the countless times I've walked into your room to find you with your nose buried in the Word. Thank you for your incredible example and for the heart you have to live a life worthy of the highest calling on earth. I love you.

Noah, my oldest son and the one most like me. If you ever wonder why the two of us struggle sometimes, it's because we are so much alike. You are my cautious child and there is absolutely nothing wrong with that. As a matter of fact, it's one of the things I love most about you. Rules are a good thing and can keep us from much heartache. Thank you for living your life with standards. Your tender heart and sweet compassion make you a very special young man. However, Noah would not be Noah without a ball of some sort in your hand. I love to watch you play, but even more than that, I love to beat you in a driveway game of H–O–R–S–E. I know . . . it's only happened once! I love you.

Eli, my John Wayne wannabe! Having never had brothers, I will never understand your love of mud and guns, but I'm learning that it's okay. I love the way you always offer to kill our Thanksgiving turkey and cook it on an open fire. Your knowledge of how things work and your curiosity about everything from wildlife to jet planes makes you quite an interesting little guy. Your sweet smile is a daily reminder that God is good. Thank you for the way you make us laugh. I love you.

Chloe, my youngest and a princess in the making. I love watching you waddle around in high heels and lipstick. You are quite the fashion diva. It's so much fun to watch you learn. You are a sweet mixture of all your siblings and are growing into a beautiful young girl. I love your spunk and your love of life. I can't imagine the day when you no longer want to crawl into your favorite pink pj's and snuggle up close for girl time. I will always cherish those times. I love you.

My heavenly Father, the Giver of all good things. I love the fact that I've never had to wander around aimlessly on this journey. The One who called me to teach my children at home is the same One who has equipped me to stay the course. You have experienced every heartache and celebration right along with me. I thank You that wherever this journey leads us and for whatever period of time we continue on it, You go before me. I'm in awe of Your love for me and Your grace extended to me. Thank you for the best students a teacher could ever ask for. Above all else, my prayer is that they learn from You, the ultimate Teacher, and the Lover of their souls. I love you.

PART ONE

Ingredients for a healthy lunch

Introduction

Sharing my lunch with you

Sometimes the only way to learn something in life is to live it out for yourself. All the reading, all the research, and all the interviews with others many times come up short in helping us understand the nitty gritty of a particular subject.

Such was the case when I began rolling around the thought of home schooling our children. After all, I had attended public schools my entire adolescent life and felt that I received a good education. I knew of others who home schooled their children and, quite frankly, I found them a little odd. Why would I want to pursue such an endeavor?

Everyone I asked about home schooling gave me a different opinion or perspective. No one could tell me exactly what the experience would entail. I frantically searched for all the reading materials I could get my hands on. I needed as much information as possible before committing to such a controversial form of education for my children.

While there were many books about the subject, I failed to find one that would provide a framework for what to expect and how to make my home school a success. That was nearly twelve years ago, but I still remember thinking to myself, "I wish there was a single book to provide me with the ins and outs of home schooling."

The book you are holding in your hands is my attempt to make your home school journey a little easier. You don't have to approach this new way of life blindly. I certainly don't consider myself the expert on home schooling; however, I have learned many lessons over the years and want to share those with others who are in the trenches. The things I share in this book are the very things I was searching for when I first began contemplating home schooling.

Each chapter will detail a particular ingredient of a successful home school, followed by a look at how that ingredient is supported in Scripture. Because our subject matter revolves around education, each chapter ends with a homework assignment. That's right! As teachers, we're much more accustomed to assigning homework than we are to having it assigned to us. However, I am a firm believer that it's easy to read something and never put what we've read into action. By including a homework assignment in each chapter, my hope is that you will incorporate many of the strategies outlined in this book. These are the principles I have used over the years to home school our four children.

Thank you for allowing me to share my experiences with you. My prayer is that you, too, will learn to enjoy the home school journey.

CHAPTER I

Lay a firm foundation

Understanding why you home school

"The rain came down, the streams rose,
and the winds blew and beat against that house;
yet it did not fall, because it had its foundation
on the rock."

Matthew 7:25 (NIV)

Whether we are building a sand castle at the beach, participating in an intense game of Jenga, or beginning work on our dream home, the key to the success of any building project is a firm foundation. The same is true when it comes to building a lasting, effective, God-centered home school to train and teach our children. It is not something we just wake up one day and decide to do. On the contrary, if your story is anything like mine, the decision to home school your children was one bathed in prayer and careful consideration. The process is so much more than choosing a curriculum and staying committed to teach that curriculum for the next nine months. Before moving forward with daily lesson plans and buying new pencils and notebooks, we first must lay a firm foundation. In other words, we must clearly understand why we home school and what we hope to accomplish by taking on such a huge responsibility.

For my husband and me, we prayed and sought God's direction long before we purchased our first preschool workbook. While we knew that God was leading us to school our children at home, we unfortunately proceeded without answers to several crucial questions. One of the most important being why we were home schooling. While God called us to home school and we were sure of that, we still needed more specific answers to the why. You see, we did not realize it at the time, but a time would come when we no longer felt the excitement and enthusiasm we felt initially. We would question if home schooling was really right for our family. We would wrestle with the thought that maybe public school would be a better fit for our kids. I am not talking about just a bad day. I am talking about when the bad days are far outweighing the good days and we wonder what we were thinking to ever embark on this journey called home schooling.

Surprisingly, we did not face this crossroad until my oldest child was entering sixth grade. The prior year had been anything but enjoyable. She was miserable. I was miserable. As a result, there was an intense feeling of dread and boredom when each new school day began. We finished her fifth grade year totally exhausted, both physically and emotionally. I really was not sure what the next year would hold. It was that summer that my Bible study group decided to study the book of John. It sounded good to me. I was frazzled and needed a refreshing washing in the Word. Somehow I just knew that God was going to release me from the call of home schooling. I decided to get a jumpstart on my new education plan. I called various private schools to get tuition costs and to better understand their teaching philosophies. I checked into public schools and searched their ratings and teacher credentials. I was not sure which direction the Lord would lead us, but I was certain it would not be the home school route.

As I began reading the book of John that summer I was also earnestly praying that God would somehow give me a clear direction for our upcoming school year. By week five of the study, I was reading a passage in the tenth chapter of the book of John that I had read countless times in the past. However, this time I saw something totally unexpected. Verses eleven through thirteen read, *"I am the Good Shepherd. The Good Shepherd puts the sheep before himself, sacrifices himself if necessary. A hired man is not a real shepherd. The sheep mean nothing to him. He sees a wolf come and runs for it, leaving the sheep to be ravaged and scattered by the wolf. He's only in it for the money. The sheep don't matter to him."* (MSG)

In that instant God revealed to me that I was like the Good Shepherd in this passage, and the hired man was likened to the public school teacher. Who has more of a vested interest in my sheep, my children? Of course, I do. Many times a hired teacher views teaching as a job. As a parent, it is so much more than that. It is a high calling with eternal rewards. Please do not misunderstand me here. I am well aware that there are countless teachers who truly care about their students and take their jobs seriously. They do a great job imparting knowledge to their classrooms of students and creating within those students a greater hunger to learn. I know many such teachers and applaud them all for a job well done. However, I am also fully aware that no one cares for my children and their educational success more than I do. There is no teacher, whether in the public or private sector, that will go the distance with my children that I will. There is no teacher who has the same vested interest in my children as I do.

Jesus preaches on the importance of a firm foundation

Jesus closed His Sermon on the Mount with a vivid comparison between a life built on a sure foundation and one hastily put together on a foundation of sand. Matthew 7:24-

27 (NIV) says, "*Therefore everyone who hears these words of mine and puts them into practice is like a wise man who built his house on the rock. The rain came down, the streams rose, and the winds blew and beat against that house; yet it did not fall, because it had its foundation on the rock. But everyone who hears these words of mine and does not put them into practice is like a foolish man who built his house on sand. The rain came down, the streams rose, and the winds blew and beat against that house, and it fell with a great crash.*"

If we look closely at Jesus' teaching in this passage of Scripture, we quickly learn that a solid foundation is imperative to anything we do. That is especially true of our decision to home school. The winds and rains Jesus refers to may not be literal, but they certainly do exist within the context of home schooling. Maybe we do not have to walk around with pop-up umbrellas and wind breakers, but we can still certainly expect to weather some serious storms. What happens when we begin to get questioned by family and friends about the pitfalls of home schooling? What happens when our kids are struggling to learn and we begin to feel responsible for their failures? Or, maybe our kids are excelling academically, but struggling to feel accepted by their peers. What do we do then? Better yet, what if it all hits at once, much like a violent storm with high winds and record amounts of rain? Do we cower and run for cover, or do we remain steadfast because our decision to home school was not flippant, but was instead based on a solid belief in and strategy for success? The Word is clear that we will face storms; the question is will we endure the storm or will everything we have worked so hard for come down with a great crash!

The answer to that question depends on one thing, our foundation. A strong foundation can endure the questions and criticism from well-meaning family and friends; however, a compromised foundation will crumble. So, how do we make sure that our foundation is one that will last? The same way a builder lays a solid foundation for an impressive building. The deeper the foundation, the stronger the structure. Digging a deep foundation requires much time and hard work. It is not completed in a day.

The same holds true in our decision to home school. That one decision must be made after much time and effort. We must take time to diligently pray about the decision and seek God's will for our families. There is also time involved in researching the world of home schooling and all it encompasses, everything from curriculum choices to teaching styles. We must answer some very basic questions such as, "Why do I home school?" and "What will home schooling look like for our family?" The answers to these questions are very personal and differ from family to family. However, with every question we are able to answer in advance of embarking on the home school journey the deeper our foundation will be and the better we will weather the storm.

I believe every home school parent has those days when we throw our hands in the air, fall to our knees in tears, and ask ourselves what we could have possibly been thinking when we signed on to educate our children at home. It is times like these when we remember our foundation and remind ourselves of everything we know to be true about this incredibly high calling.

Homework

Begin thinking about your decision to home school your children. If you are contemplating a home-based education for the very first time, talk it over with your spouse. Interview others who educate their children at home. Pray and ask for God's wisdom and direction. I encourage you to put some things on paper. List your reasons for wanting to home school, list your concerns, and list your goals. Take time to define what your home school will look like. Just as you would for any other important endeavor, put together an all-inclusive plan. Create a tangible document that serves to guide you in the days, weeks, months, and even years ahead.

Maybe you are a seasoned veteran home schooler, but have never taken the time to think through the reasons why you do what you do. Now is a great time to do just that. Put a plan in place so that when, not if, those difficult school days bring you down and cause you to question your efforts, you can be reminded of all the reasons you chose to home school your children in the first place.

CHAPTER 2

Understand learning differences

Identifying your child's learning style

"Your hands made me and formed me; give me
understanding to learn your commands."
Psalm 119:73 (NIV)

With four children it did not take me long to realize that what worked for one of them did not necessarily work for the other. In the beginning it was quite frustrating. I purchased curriculum that allowed me to combine several subjects, such as history and science, so that I could teach my two oldest children at the same time. They would work independently in math, language and spelling, but we would all come together to study the Civil War and mammals. It sounded like a logical plan to me and I looked forward to making the most of my time during the school day. Not far into the school year I realized that the time I spent teaching those combined subjects was some of the most frustrating time of my entire day. Our curriculum was pretty straightforward. Basically I would read the lesson aloud and ask oral questions about what I had read. The children would answer the questions orally and then follow-up with some sort of activity to reinforce the information learned.

My oldest daughter had very little trouble when it came time for the oral review. She answered questions quickly and accurately. My son, however, gave me a blank stare whenever I would direct a question at him. He responded as if he had never heard of the information contained in the review questions. First, I would scratch my head and wonder if I had only dreamed that I just finished twenty minutes of reading aloud to my kids. Then, I would surmise that my son obviously was not listening during the reading time. He was unable to answer even the most basic questions from the day's chapter. I lectured him on the importance of being attentive and engaged during the daily reading time.

None of my tactics worked. I then decided that maybe it would help if he were allowed to draw while I read. His assignment was to draw a picture to illustrate what I was reading each day. At the end of our reading time he had a great piece of artwork, but was still unable to answer a single question about what he had learned. I was fairly new to home schooling at this point and found myself becoming extremely frustrated about our combined study times.

It was not until much later that year that I heard about the importance of identifying your child's learning style. I began educating myself about the way children learn, and I could not believe what I was discovering. My oldest daughter learned best by hearing information presented. She is an auditory learner. My oldest son is a visual learner. He prefers reading things for himself, seeing them on paper, and studying them. No wonder my daughter was excelling while my son was struggling during our daily history and science lessons. This discovery was like a breath of fresh air to me. So many things began to make sense. No longer would I read long history lessons aloud to my son. Instead, I would hand him the book and allow him to do the reading on his own. It was amazing to me how easily he was then able to answer review questions. The solution all along was to properly identify how my son preferred to learn. Once we were able to do that, learning became much easier for him.

So what is a learning style and how do you figure out which learning style best describes your child? Basically, learning styles refer to the way in which a person gathers information. Although most people take in information in several ways, each person generally has a preferred learning style. For school-aged children the best learning takes place when information is presented in a way that activates their preferred style. When children are taught via modes that do not activate their preferred style, learning can be inhibited.

There are three basic learning styles: auditory, visual and kinesthetic. These styles determine a child's ability to acquire, process and store information. Most children have one of the three learning styles as their dominant style, but are able to learn to a lesser degree when information is presented using one of the other, less-dominant learning styles.

There is much to learn and explore when it comes to children and how they learn. However, a basic understanding of each learning style can help you identify which style best fits your child. The auditory learner learns best by using their sense of hearing. They prefer lectures and read-alouds when new information is being presented. The visual learner prefers to gather information using their sense of sight. They enjoy slide shows, movies, charts, and graphs. The child who is a kinesthetic learner prefers to be taught using the hands-on approach. They like to touch and feel, and they learn best when manipulatives are used to teach new information.

Many children are a combination of two or more learning styles. The key is to observe your child, question them, and give them ample opportunity to learn using each of the three learning styles. Before long you will be able to identify your child's dominant style. Once you know how your child best likes to learn, you can tailor your curriculum and teaching style to optimize your child's learning.

Noah, doubting Thomas, and a tax collector possess various learning styles

One of the greatest examples of a man who learned best by processing information through his sense of hearing was Noah. You will recall from Genesis chapters six through nine that God planned to destroy all living things with a flood. In preparation for this flood, He gave Noah very specific instructions for building an ark to save him and his family.

In Genesis 6:15-16 (NIV), God says, "*This is how you are to build it: The ark is to be three hundred cubits long, fifty cubits wide and thirty cubits high. Make a roof for it, leaving below the roof an opening one cubit high all around. Put a door in the side of the ark and make lower, middle and upper decks.*" We never read that Noah asked God to write the directions down for him or to demonstrate for him exactly how to shape the roof or where to put the door. Noah did not scribble down measurements as God spoke to him concerning plans for the ark. He simply listened and did what God asked him to do. Genesis 6:22 (NIV) says, "*Noah did everything just as God commanded him.*"

For us visual learners, this could have been a nightmare. We would have needed a detailed drawing done to scale with every measurement clearly labeled and color coded. A simple set of audible instructions would have put us in a tailspin.

The kinesthetic learner would have needed to practice first by building a three-dimensional desktop model of the ark. Just hearing the specific measurements of the ark would not have motivated us to action. We would actually have to handle the cypress wood and experiment with different building techniques before the first board was ever fitted into place.

But Noah was different. God knew that he would be able to hear the instructions and build the ark precisely according to God's directions. Surely Noah was an auditory learner who processed information quickly and easily through his sense of hearing.

Then there was Thomas, one of Jesus' twelve disciples, who was really better known as Doubting Thomas. He was given this label because he simply did not believe that Jesus had risen from the dead. We learn in the book of John that after Jesus' resurrection, He appeared to some of the disciples, but Thomas was not with them at the time. John 20:25 (NIV) says, *"Unless I see the nail marks in his hands and put my finger where the nails were, and put my hand into his side, I will not believe it."*

A week later Jesus' disciples, including Thomas, were in the house again. According to John 20:26-27 (NIV), Jesus appeared through locked doors and stood among them saying, *"Peace be with you!"* Then he said to Thomas,

"*Put your finger here, see my hands. Reach out your hand and put it into my side.*" Jesus was challenging Thomas to stop doubting and start believing. But in order to do that, Thomas would need to physically touch Jesus' nail-scarred hands and feel his side. For the other disciples, it was enough to simply see Jesus on his first visit. But Thomas could not believe until he had actually touched Jesus. I have to believe that Thomas was a kinesthetic learner.

The same would hold true if we had a child who was a kinesthetic learner, and we tried to teach them basic arithmetic facts by verbalizing the facts over and over. While learning would probably eventually take place, a much more efficient means of teaching the same material would be to use some sort of math manipulative. Instead of verbalizing random addition facts, we could hand our first-grader blocks, pennies, or even Matchbox cars to count. With a kinesthetic learner, this kind of teaching would accomplish much more in a much shorter period of time.

Let us now turn our attention to the third and final learning style and a rich, chief tax collector named Zacchaeus. The nineteenth chapter of Luke tells us that Jesus had entered Jericho and was passing through the city when a large crowd gathered around him. Zacchaeus was vertically challenged and struggled to catch a glimpse of the Man everyone wanted to see. He quickly located a nearby tree and made his way to the top in order to see Jesus. You have probably heard this story and already know the ending. Jesus spotted Zacchaeus in the top limbs and called for him to come down. Luke 19:5 (ESV) says, *"Zacchaeus, hurry and come down; for I must stay at your house today."*

For Zacchaeus it was not enough to hear about Jesus coming through town. He was most likely a visual learner, someone who processes information best using their sense of sight. Zacchaeus needed to see Jesus for himself. He could not process how he felt about Jesus or what he perceived him to be without actually looking at him, studying him.

The same thing holds true with students who are visual learners. If they are learning state capitals in geography, they would much rather look at a list of states and their capitals, or study a map, than listen to a teacher talk about which capital belongs to which state. They would rather study charts with rules of the English language than hear them taught aloud.

Homework

Make it your goal to determine the learning style for each of your children. Simply reading a comprehensive book on the subject can provide you with the tools you need to successfully determine how your child best likes to learn. Once you feel comfortable that you have properly identified your child's learning style then make every effort to teach to your child's style. Look for creative ways to present new information based on how your child likes to receive it. It may seem awkward at first if you are accustomed to using only one specific teaching style. Ultimately, however, you will discover that it is beneficial to both you and your child. Learning becomes easier and more rewarding.

CHAPTER 3

Navigate the curriculum chaos

*Choosing the right curriculum
for your children*

─────────────

"If any of you lacks wisdom, you should ask God,
who gives generously to all without finding fault,
and it will be given to you."

James 1:5 (NIV)

By far, one of the most intimidating and overwhelming parts of home schooling can be settling on a curriculum to use with your children. If you have ever researched the endless textbooks and teaching tools available in the marketplace today, you no doubt quickly realized that the options are limitless. There is quite a smorgasbord of lesson plans, teaching techniques, supplies, and manipulatives to guide you in your home school efforts. There is everything from teacher-led unit studies to structured textbook resources, depending on your personal preference. The Internet provides an opportunity to explore a multitude of different curricula and teaching methods. It serves as a great first glance at the vast possibilities available. However, the best way to truly evaluate a particular curriculum and judge its appropriateness for your family is to peruse the curriculum for yourself, physically thumbing through the teaching materials, reading the assignments, and evaluating the curriculum's approach to teaching. One of the best places to do this is at a local home school conference. While there is an admission fee to these conferences, the benefits of researching several different curricula at one time far outweigh the cost. Many times these conferences offer the opportunity for you to talk to other parents who have used the curricula and can comment on their ease of use and practicality. It serves as an incredible resource to help narrow down and even determine your curriculum direction.

When we first began our home school journey eleven years ago I felt totally overwhelmed by all the resources available to me. I had no clue how to proceed and had never heard of a home school conference. I blindly chose a curriculum that I felt covered everything that my then four-year-old daughter would need and hit the trail with high aspirations. I ordered every last workbook, vowel chart, and flashcard available. There was not a supplemental resource available that I did not own. Keep in mind that my daughter was four at the time and just beginning preschool. I used that year to totally explore home schooling. My thought was the only way to really know what it would be like was to totally immerse my daughter in a full-blown preschool curriculum.

The biggest reason I chose the curriculum I did was because everything was laid out for me. From lesson plans to worksheets to answer guides, all the work had been done for me. Looking back, it probably was not a bad thing to use a structured curriculum that first year. My mistake came when I refused to explore other options in the years to come. As we added more children to the mix, along with different personalities and learning styles, I never considered researching other curricula. I am embarrassed to admit that I did not break away from that particular approach to home schooling until my daughter entered fifth grade. Even then I was reluctant to try something new. However, little by little I began incorporating new books and teaching methods until I felt like I was finally educating my children in the best way possible for them, a way that engaged them and made learning much more meaningful.

Gideon seeks direction from God

Making a wise decision is crucial, but no decision is wise if it is made independently of God. All wisdom comes from God, and learning to respond with His wisdom is a skill that takes time to develop. As we use His wisdom with even the small, seemingly insignificant decisions in our lives, when the big decisions come, we will be sensitive and aware of God's leading and His wisdom.

Gideon longed to make the right decision in the book of Judges. Because Israel was sinning against God, He sent the Midianites to rule over them. After seven long years of dealing with the Midianites, the Israelites cried out for God to save them. According to Judges 6:12 (NIV), a short time later an angel of the Lord visited with Gideon under an oak tree, saying, *"The Lord is with you mighty warrior."* Gideon's response? Basically he responded with something like, "If God is with us then why are the Midianites harming our crops and treating us badly? What happened to all those miracles that our fathers have told us about?" The angel responded by telling Gideon that God was sending him to save Israel. Gideon immediately began to make excuses, claiming that his clan was the weakest in all of Israel and that he was the weakest of his clan. He had a decision to make. Would he believe what the angel had told him or would he neglect his call because of fear of failure? Gideon responded by asking for a sign. Judges 6:36-37 (MSG) tells us that Gideon prayed to God that night saying, *"If this is right, if you are using me to save Israel as you've said, then look: I'm placing a fleece of wool on the threshing floor. If dew is on the fleece only, but the floor is dry, then I know that you will use me to save Israel, as you said."* He carefully placed a wool fleece on the ground and went to bed. The next morning, he immediately checked the fleece and found it wringing wet, while the grass around it was dry.

But his decision to believe the angel was such an important one that he again returned to God with another request. Judges 6:39 (MSG) says that he prayed that night saying, *"Don't be impatient with me, but let me say one more thing. I want to try another time with the fleece. But this time let the fleece stay dry, while the dew drenches the ground."* Again, he carefully placed the wool fleece on the ground and went to bed. When he awoke the next morning, he found the fleece perfectly dry and the ground around it saturated. At this point, he knew it was true. God was going to use him to save Israel.

Some have chastised Gideon for the way he questioned what God was asking him to do. Others find it comforting to know that God cared enough to confirm His call on Gideon's life more than once. Either way, Gideon had a decision to make and he wanted to be sure he was hearing from God.

Choosing a home school curriculum may seem trivial in light of the story of Gideon. After all, it is not like we are setting about to save a nation. However, God sees it as important. Just as He confirmed Gideon's decision in the book of Judges, ask Him to lead you and set your mind clear on the resources He would have you use in your home school.

Homework

Do some research. With the Internet at our fingertips today, the access we have to information is mind-boggling at times. However, use this information to your benefit. Join online home school discussion groups and listen to what others are saying about the curriculum they use. Contact curricula suppliers and request free catalogs so that you can peruse the wide variety of resources for yourself. Do not forget to look for materials specifically created for your child's learning style. By all means, find a way to attend a home school conference in your area. No amount of research can substitute for seeing the curriculum in person, thumbing through its pages, and studying the accompanying teacher resources. If at all possible, have your children join you. Their input can be invaluable. Most importantly, pray for God's direction in choosing your curriculum. The tools you use to teach can be the difference between an incredible home school experience and a seemingly hopeless attempt at survival. Take the time to do your homework. I can promise you will be glad you did.

CHAPTER 4

Create a workable schedule

Discovering freedom in planning

"Many are the plans in a person's heart,
but it is the LORD's purpose that prevails."

Proverbs 19:21 (NIV)

I know, I know. Many people hear the word "schedule" and automatically retreat to defense mode, claiming that they do not operate that way and instead prefer to let the day unfold as it may. The thought of having their day mapped out before it even begins leaves some people rolling their eyes and wondering how others survive in such a structured environment. Charts and schedules tend to take the fun and spontaneity out of the day for many home school moms.

However, I must admit that I have been on the opposite end of the spectrum from those moms. I have operated at the far extreme when it comes to scheduling our day. To our detriment, at times I have scheduled our day with such tenacity that it left little, if any, room for flexibility. Within a week of finishing up our school year, I was already working on the next year's schedule. I do not mean I was thinking about what curriculum I would use or what approach I would use to teaching. I was literally planning, minute by minute, our school days. To say I was a slave to our schedule would be an understatement. It was such an integral part of our day that if one of my children woke up sick or we had an unexpected visitor or phone call, I would be swept into a tailspin. I simply went to pieces and considered the day a failure. In my opinion, if the schedule did not work completely, the schedule did not work.

Proverbs 16:9 (NASB) says, *"The mind of man plans his way, but the Lord directs his steps."* I was doing an incredible job of planning my way, but I was totally unreceptive to allowing the Lord to direct my steps. That, I believe, is the difference in a schedule that enables you to stay focused and one that prohibits productivity. I was desperately struggling to keep my eyes on the goal each day. My poor children suffered right along with me, just trying to keep on task and follow the schedule. We actually became slaves to the thing I had hoped would bring order and peace to our day.

Once I began realizing that my obsession with a detailed schedule was robbing us of many of the joys afforded to home school families, it was up to me to do something about it. I would like to say that I simply dropped the schedule and we operated at a more leisurely pace; however, that would be less than the truth. You see, planning and scheduling had been a part of who I was for as long as I could remember. Even as a child, I was always making task lists and scheduling my days. I am even guilty of putting a reminder on my list to take a shower, just so that I could mark it off. It gave me a real sense of accomplishment to see all those checked-off items at the end of my day. I know what you are probably thinking, "She really needed some sort of therapy as a child." You may be right, but I never thought of it as unusual, and I continued to be a very detailed, organized student throughout high school and college. I simply loved the sense of satisfaction it gave me when I looked back over all I had accomplished. Once I had children, I continued to plan and schedule my days between work and family. It was a challenge, but I found a system that worked and it felt good. However, when we decided to follow God's call to home school our children, it never occurred to me that my own flesh and blood would not be as excited about a daily schedule as I was. I vomited my gift of organization and love of flow charts all over them and they were less than enthusiastic, to say the least. I am embarrassed to admit that it was not until my oldest daughter was entering ninth grade that I finally found a system that I felt successfully guided us through our day without hindering our enthusiasm for what we were doing. It was a huge compromise for me and one I am still learning to put into practice. I am still an organization freak at heart; however, I am discovering that there is real freedom in some degree of flexibility.

Do I still have a schedule for each child for each school year? Absolutely! Does that schedule begin at 6:30 a.m. and end at bedtime, detailing every event for a particular day in thirty-minute time segments? Certainly not! I have tried to find my way back to the center of the pendulum where there is a healthy balance. I know families who stick to a rigid daily schedule and do it well. I know others who laugh at the very thought of having a schedule and operate just fine with no set plan for the day. However, for the Vance family, we now operate somewhere in between. I am a firm believer that a daily schedule can help bring structure and order to the day. It does not have to be detailed, just functional.

Nehemiah has a plan for rebuilding

If you spent much time at all in Sunday School as a child you are probably very familiar with the story of Nehemiah. Basically, Nehemiah was heartbroken that the city of Jerusalem was still in shambles, even after the return of the first exiles in 538 B.C. and a second group in 458 B.C. Along with God's persuasion, he personally assumed the responsibility of rebuilding the city walls. He walked away from an important position as cupbearer to the Persian king and pursued the passion God had placed in his heart. Nehemiah had no background in rallying a group of people for a common cause. Nowhere will you read that Nehemiah had extensive background in organizing major building projects. He was not known for any prior experience as a construction site manager. Yet, not only did Nehemiah accomplish the seemingly impossible task of rebuilding the city walls, but he did so in a staggering fifty-two days. Wow! We hear that story and wonder how someone like Nehemiah pulled it off. After all, rebuilding the walls of Jerusalem was no easy task. A large part of his success came in the form of being organized. In the third chapter of Nehemiah we learn that Nehemiah organized the people into groups and assigned them to specific sections of the wall. In other words, he had a plan. Eliashib worked to rebuild the Sheep Gate; the Fish Gate was rebuilt by the sons of Hassenaah; the Jeshanah Gate was repaired by Joiada and Meshullam; the Valley Gate was repaired by Hanun and the residents of Zanoah; etc. Most likely Nehemiah did not have a color-coded spreadsheet outlining each builder's job assignment, but he did have a plan nonetheless. Not only did each builder have an assigned portion of the wall to rebuild, but each was also responsible for the part of the wall closest to his house. Why would Nehemiah choose to approach such a huge project this way? Why did he require each builder to not only take care of his section of the wall, but also those sections closest to his? Perhaps it was an experiment in time management. I am sure Nehemiah had several reasons for making this a requirement. However, I have to believe that at least part of his reason was to promote efficiency. If each builder had the added responsibility of rebuilding the wall in front of his own house, he would not waste time traveling to more distant parts of the wall. Thus, the work on the wall could be completed sooner rather than later.

Homework

A schedule really does for us the same thing it was able to do for Nehemiah. It allows us to move through our days in an orderly fashion, making the best use of our time. Can it be done without a schedule? Quite certainly. People do it every day. However, can we work more efficiently and effectively if we have a guide for our day? I believe we can. If you have never taken the time to develop a plan for your school days I encourage you to give it a try. It does not have to be elaborate, printed on colored cardstock paper, and laminated. Just scribble out a tentative plan for your day, and do your best to follow it. It can be as simple as a list of those main things you want you and your children to achieve for the day.

If you have tried a schedule in the past without success, I encourage you to give it another shot. Think about what caused your schedule to fail the last time. Was it too detailed? Maybe it did not offer enough information.

Did you allow room for flexibility? How about getting input from your children about what they would like to see happen during your typical school day together? Once you have identified past problem areas, put your pen to paper once again and work to improve your schedule so that it meets the needs of your family and enables you to make the most of your time at home.

CHAPTER 5

Hasten to offer praise

*Motivating your children
with heartfelt praise*

———⟊⟊⟊———

"Therefore encourage one another and build
each other up, just as in fact you are doing."

1 Thessalonians 5:11 (NIV)

If there is anything I have learned over the last eleven years of home schooling, it is the importance of praising my children. For far too long I operated under the premise that if I said nothing at all it was the same as saying, "You are doing a great job!" I made comments only when there was a problem or I noticed some character flaw that I felt the need to address. As a result I was consistently offering negative feedback without ever verbalizing the good qualities I saw in my children. This really did not occur to me until my oldest son was given a personality test. The test revealed many things about him that my husband and I found interesting. However, the one thing that stood out most to me was the fact that he needed specific praise. In other words, not only did he need to hear positive feedback, but that feedback needed to be very specific. Saying, "Good job!" to my son was the same as saying nothing at all. He needed to hear, "Nice job on your math test. You studied hard and double-checked your work. Your diligence really paid off." Or, "I am very proud of the way you helped your brother with his work. Thank you for practicing patience with him." It is amazing to watch his face light up when he receives praise. The same is true of all my children. They love to know that I am proud of them and value their hard work. Is that not true of most people? We all like to hear that we are appreciated and are doing a good job. However, for some reason we are much quicker to offer judgment and condemnation than we are encouragement.

Not only do my children enjoy receiving praise, but I have also found that it motivates them to work harder. Whereas negativity kills their spirits, encouragement causes their spirits to soar. It sounds so easy, and we all know the importance of providing positive reinforcement, but still it is easy to get so busy that we forget to take the time to bless others with our words.

While we commonly think of encouragement in terms of the words we use, we cannot underestimate the power of prayer. One of the best ways to encourage our children is to talk to God about them. When my kids are struggling with certain attitudes or behaviors, I look for specific Scriptures to pray over them. Who better than God Himself to strengthen my children and help them understand their value and worth? When I am discouraged I want other people praying for me. The same goes for my children. What better way to encourage our precious gifts from God than to ask the Creator of the universe to protect their hearts and minds?

Aaron and Hur provide a lesson in encouragement

In Exodus 17 we see Israel faced with its first major military threat, a hostile tribe known as the Amalekites. As they engaged in combat, Moses prayed for his army with his arms outstretched, just as he had done when he faced the Red Sea. His prayers served as a covering for his people. While his arms were held high, holding the staff, the Israelites were winning the battle, but when Moses became weak and his arms began to fall, the enemy began to prevail. Exodus 17:11 (MSG) says, *"It turned out that whenever Moses raised his hands, Israel was winning, but whenever he lowered his hands, Amalek was winning."* However, after a while, Moses' arms became so tired that he could no longer hold them up on his own. Since an uplifted arm can only be raised so long, and the outcome of the battle depended on Moses' ability to pray with outstretched arms, two of his right-hand men stepped up to support their leader. Verse twelve says, *"So they got a stone and set it under him. He sat on it and Aaron and Hur held up his hands, one on each side."*

The book of Exodus goes on to say that Aaron and Hur held Moses' hands steady until sunset, and the Israelites were eventually victorious over the Amalekites. Moses needed encouragement because these "stiff-necked" people were complaining and criticizing him. His intercession proved to be the difference between victory and defeat in battle that day. The physical and mental strength of the Israelite army was not what won the battle, but it was the power of prayer. The hilltop overlooking the battlefield was where the battle was truly won.

Aaron and Hur gave Moses encouragement and support, something we all need. Some days your kids just do not want to do school. Maybe they are tired or feeling discouraged. They may be dreading an upcoming math test or do not particularly care for the book report book they are reading. Perhaps they are struggling with a friendship or questioning their relationship with God. A host of circumstances and situations can cause us to feel discouraged, unmotivated, or even sad. Guess what? We all have days like that. Everyone needs people like Aaron and Hur to lift them up in prayer. Our kids need to hear us say, "You are doing an amazing job, but I am here for you if you get stuck or need help." Remember, when the arms get tired, the work slows down.

I love the ending to this story about Moses. In recognition of the victory over the Amalekites, Moses erects an altar as a reminder of how God intervened on behalf of the Israelites. This was a type of victory monument, showing that when Moses covered his people in prayer, God covered them with divine protection. As we provide our children with the support and encouragement they need, we too are erecting monuments, living monuments that proclaim God's faithfulness.

Homework

As believers we are called to support the hurting, the discouraged, the lost, the frustrated, the weak, and the helpless. What we sometimes fail to recognize is that many times those people are our very own children. We are quick to support the local food pantry or volunteer to teach a Bible study, but oftentimes we neglect to follow through on some of the most basic acts of Christian service, such as offering a word of encouragement to a third-grader struggling with their multiplication tables.

Your assignment is pretty straightforward. Discover ways to encourage your children. Make it your goal to find at least one opportunity to praise your child daily. Of course, more than once a day is even better. Experiment and see if maybe your child, too, needs specific edification. You may be praising them, but they may not be receiving it. If you want to take it a step further, you may want to consider personality tests for your children. These tests will help you know how your children like to receive praise. Above all else, offer encouragement through prayer. Make it a daily practice to pray for your children. Just as Moses' hands grew tired, our children can grow weary and need the prayer support of their parents.

CHAPTER 6

Begin each day anew

Accepting grace on your worst days

—◦◦❀◦◦—

"Hear my cry for mercy as I call to you for help,
as I lift up my hands toward your Most Holy Place."

Psalm 28:2 (NIV)

How many times have I blown it with my kids only to still be beating myself up over it a week later? It usually happens when I have worked extra hard to plan our school day. All necessary copies have been made in advance, all needed science experiment supplies are bought and on-hand, textbooks and reference books are properly stored in their respective "homes", pencils are sharpened, and the notebook paper tray is abundantly stocked. Everything imaginable has been done ahead of time to ensure a successful school day. It is usually on those days, days when my expectations are unusually high, that my kids awake with little motivation for the day. They simply are not as excited about school as I would like them to be. After several unsuccessful attempts to pump them full of energy and excitement, I succumb to the fact that I am the only one even remotely energized enough to tackle the day. This realization, along with my children's lackadaisical attitudes, often proves to be more than I can handle. Before I know it, all my good intentions and well-laid plans go out the window, along with my love, joy, peace, patience, kindness, goodness, faithfulness, gentleness and self-control – all those qualities that I am supposed to possess as a child of God. I end up being short with my kids and irritable toward my husband who is not even home. I find myself with a bad attitude, doing the bare minimum just to get through the day. My desire for excellence in our school day is quickly replaced by a goal to simply SURVIVE the day. At that point, I am really not doing anyone any good. Ultimately, I close out the day wrapped in a blanket of guilt for how little we accomplished and the poor attitude I displayed toward others, especially my family.

Most people could take that day and chalk it up to experience. The lesson learned? Do not set your goals so high that you fall apart when you miss the mark. However, it has never been that easy for me. I could never seem to just get a good night's sleep and start all over in the morning. For the longest time, I would awaken the next morning still feeling like a failure from the day before. I would crawl out of bed with the same destructive emotions that haunted me when I crawled into bed the night before. I would approach the day expecting the worst. No matter how well-behaved my children were that day, or how much we were able to accomplish, I still carried around the guilt from the disastrous day before. Not only that, but many times I was still nursing those feelings a week later. I could not see all the good days in our home school journey for focusing too much on the few days that were mediocre, at best.

For me, the solution was two-fold. First of all, I had to stop setting unrealistic expectations. I have four children at home, ranging in age from five to fifteen. Something is bound to go wrong in the course of our day. We live in a modest home and find ourselves in very close physical proximity to one another for much of the day. If nothing else, the lack of space can sometimes cause irritations among otherwise loving family members. I cannot count how many times I have heard, "Your foot is touching me!" or "Your elbow is in my way!" After spending six or seven hours together in tight quarters, we many times find ourselves grumbling and complaining. To complicate matters, I have a goal to complete a certain amount of work with each child daily, and, I must admit, my goals are pretty lofty. Some might even term them "over the top." It took me nearly ten years of home schooling to realize that what I was striving for was not excellence, like I had tried to convince myself, but instead it was a desire to impress others. I never wanted people to question whether or not my kids were getting a good education. I never wanted neighbors to think that my kids did not understand work ethic or diligence. And, heaven forbid that my kids would go through life with sub-par scores on their school records because they could not master standardized achievement tests. Sooner or later someone would see those scores and then what? When I finally realized that my home school strategy had become centered on what others thought, I quickly recognized my so-called goals for what they really were – PRIDE. What? Could putting together great lesson plans and organizing an aggressive strategy to teach my children really be considered pride? Yes. You mean it is prideful to want the very best for my kids? It can be if my motivation is being compromised. The work I do to ensure a great school day, in and of itself, is perfectly fine. However, the problem becomes evident when I examine my motives. Why do I put together such elaborate plans and push my kids to complete advanced academic studies on a daily basis? Naturally, I want them to have a solid academic foundation to enable them to complete higher-education training in the future. But, at the heart of it all is the need to prove myself to those around me, many of whom are strangers. Proverbs 16:18 (NKJV) tells us that "*pride goes before destruction, and a haughty spirit before a fall.*" I have read that verse in the Bible countless times, but was ignorant of the fact that a haughty spirit was the driving force behind everything I was doing. After all, who wants to admit that they are in an all-out war against the foe of pride? However, when I looked at the definition of pride in Webster's, I could not deny the obvious. Pride is defined as a delight or elation arising from some act, possession, or relationship. That described me precisely. I was finding great satisfaction in my elaborate home school plans and the amount of work my kids were completing every day. Who cares that we were all getting burnt out? Who cares that we viewed school as an assignment to be endured every day, but never enjoyed? Did it really matter that by the time 5:00 p.m. rolled around every afternoon, we were physically and mentally drained, interested in nothing but time away from one another and a full night's sleep? Absolutely! Not only did it matter, but I quickly realized that I was killing my kids' love of learning. School was something to be dreaded and put off for as long as possible. Is that really the goal I had in mind when I first started home schooling? Of course not. Pride had successfully twisted my thinking and reasoning until I could no longer even remember why I home schooled in the first place. Was this really what I had signed up for? The solution? Go back to the plan. Remember, one of the first things you want to do before teaching your children their first math lesson is to lay a firm foundation, outlining why you want to home school and the goals you have for your children and their educations.

Jeremiah understands God's mercies

After the death of King Josiah, the last righteous king, the nation of Judah had almost completely abandoned God and His commandments. God had promised that He would judge idolatry most severely, and Jeremiah had warned Judah of God's judgment. As a result of Judah's continued and unrepentant idolatry, God allowed the Babylonians to besiege, plunder, burn, and destroy the city of Jerusalem. Solomon's Temple, which had stood for approximately 400 years, was burned to the ground. The book of Lamentations reveals the mourning of Jeremiah over the destruction of Jerusalem. Jeremiah speaks of unimaginable suffering on the part of the people for their involvement in rampant idolatry. Nevertheless, he does not focus on the suffering. Instead, he consoles both himself and the people with images of the character of God, namely His mercy. In the same way, God does not want us focus on the negative aspects of our lives. He does not want us to live in regret of all we have done wrong or the countless times we have fallen short of His glory. Nor does He want us to beat ourselves up every time we have a sub-standard school day with our children. Granted, He wants us to learn from our mistakes and make every effort to shore up those areas where we struggle; however, we do not have to carry that burden with us for days and weeks to come. It was because of God's great mercy in the book of Lamentations that the people were not utterly consumed. Jeremiah specifically points out that God's mercies are new every morning. Lamentations 3:21-24 (NIV) says, *"Yet this I call to mind and therefore I have hope: because of the LORD's great love we are not consumed, for his compassions never fail. They are new every morning; great is your faithfulness."* His mercies are new every morning. That means we can get up every day without condemnation, knowing that we can do things differently than we did the day before. We are not forced to live in the shadow of a perfect school day that could have been. Instead, we make every effort to learn from our mistakes, accepting responsibility for failures, and move forward in pursuit of providing a quality, Christ-centered education for our children.

Homework

Just as Jeremiah chose to focus, not on the past, but on the promises of God for the days to come, we can do the same. Our assignment is to do just that – approach each day for what it truly is, a brand new day. Your homework for beginning each day anew is fairly easy in theory, but can be quite difficult to implement. All I am asking you to do is to grab a 4x6 index card and a permanent marker in some fun color that conveys life and newness. Something about words written in black marker do not have the same feel as those written in rosy red or lime green. I can understand writing a verse like, *"Thou shalt not kill"* in black, but for our purposes we want to focus on a more exciting color. So, with card and marker in hand, I would like for you to write (in your very best penmanship, of course) the verse we read from Lamentations 3:21-24. I love the Message Bible translation of this passage of Scripture, so I will ask you to write that version on your card. "*But there's one other thing I remember, and remembering, I keep a grip on hope: God's loyal love couldn't have run out, his merciful love couldn't have dried up. They're created new every morning. How great your faithfulness! I'm sticking with God (I say it over and over). He's all I've got left.*" This card will find its home on the front of your refrigerator door. However, if you are anything like me you may want to construct several copies of the Scripture to post at various locations around your home. Much of my day is spent at my desk, so I always make sure that any reminders or words of encouragement I might need during the day are in plain sight at my computer desk.

As I said, writing out Scripture on a card is easy. The hard part begins when we have one of those miserable days of feeling like a complete failure, and struggle to pull ourselves out of the pit of despair. Those are the days when the Scripture must become more than words on a page. It must become a part of who we are and what we believe to be true. We must not only read those precious words in Lamentations, but we must also act on them. Then, and only then, will we truly be able to begin each day anew.

CHAPTER 7

Optimize your efficiency

Getting the most out of your day

"And God is able to bless you abundantly,
so that in all things at all times, having all that
you need, you will abound in every good work."

2 Corinthians 9:8 (NIV)

Home schooling alone has so many challenges that anytime you can find a way to make things easier it is well worth your time to pursue it. One of the easiest, and oftentimes most beneficial, ways to bring order to your day is to organize. Especially if you are schooling more than one child, just trying to locate a sharpened pencil can rob you of precious time in your school day.

In the past I have had the pleasure of schooling my kids from a carefully designed school room that my husband added to our home. Having a designated space to work every day was a huge blessing. Everything my kids and I needed each day was at our fingertips. Markers, glue sticks, and craft supplies were all stored in plastic containers that were clearly labeled. Notebook paper, construction paper, graph paper, and any other kind of paper you could imagine were all stacked neatly in separating dividers. We had a designated pencil drawer as well, everything from No. 2 pencils to colored pencils to mechanical pencils. Workbooks and read-aloud books were easily accessible, as were encyclopedia sets, atlases, and dictionaries. Our school room was laid out with a variety of work areas so that each child had their space to read or write without interruption from others in the room. We had a set routine for turning in work as it was completed. Each child had an in-basket that they would drop finished work into, and an out-basket to pick up their next assignment. This kept things flowing. I could work with one child without having another standing around wondering what to do next. The system we had in place was a well-oiled machine. Rarely were there breakdowns in the process. My kids knew the routine and complied beautifully. We functioned this way for nearly seven years.

In December of 2006, we moved from our home, and incredible school room, in northeast Tennessee to a new home in Indianapolis, Indiana. We searched diligently for a house that would meet the needs of our large family. Finding a house big enough was not the problem. The problem was figuring out how to pay for the larger home. In the end we bought a nice house, but it was smaller than the one we moved from. However, there was a small loft that we determined would be our new school room. The next challenge was to find a way to move all the work stations and supplies from our previous school room into this new 16' x 16' loft. We crammed as much as possible into the new space and began our attempts at schooling just as we had in Tennessee. It did not take long to discover that the loft was not working out for us. I, along with our four children, spent many long hours in that loft each day trying to find a way to accomplish the things we needed to accomplish. I was frustrated. They were frustrated. The room was a complete disaster. There was no order, no routine. There was entirely too much stuff in that small room and too many people trying to function in an incredibly tight space.

After several attempts to make school work in that room we finally resigned to the fact that what worked for us back home in Tennessee was not going to work at our new home in Indiana. It was time for a new plan. Each child was moved to a desk in their rooms and minimal supplies were neatly arranged in a single storage cabinet that remained in the loft. We replaced our school book racks with nice wooden bookshelves and limited the number of books we owned. The loft was refigured to become a much-needed living space for our family. It now houses our games, the Wii, and television. It serves as a great hangout room for the family.

My initial fear was that we could no longer operate efficiently with such little space. However, I quickly discovered that we could do all the same things we had always done, just on a smaller scale. We still have designated storage locations for craft supplies, pencils, and paper. However, we keep a much smaller supply these days. There is now one central basket on my desk for each child to pick up and drop off work. If someone walked into our house today they probably would not be able to tell that our kids are home schooled. We simply do not have much extra space so we use what space we do have as living areas. The majority of school supplies are neatly tucked away in desks and cabinets throughout the house. I do not mean that things are scattered around everywhere. I simply mean that everything has its place and my kids know what those places are. Because of that, we can function with great efficiency throughout the day.

Joseph efficiently manages resources in Egypt

If we begin reading the Bible from the beginning, it does not take long to discover the importance of efficiency. Genesis chapter forty-one gives the account of Joseph and Pharaoh. Joseph interprets Pharaoh's dreams and foretells the coming famine. He explains that there would be seven years of great abundance, followed by seven years of famine in the land of Egypt. Joseph then challenges Pharaoh to look for a discerning and wise man to put in charge of the land. Joseph instructs Pharaoh in Genesis 41:35-36 (NIV) saying, "*They should collect all the food of these good years that are coming and store up the grain under the authority of Pharaoh, to be kept in the cities for food. This food should be held in reserve for the country, to be used during the seven years of famine that will come upon Egypt, so that the country may not be ruined by the famine.*"

Pharaoh liked the plan and decided that Joseph fit the bill. He was a wise and discerning man and was put in charge of the entire land of Egypt. The people of Egypt were given instructions to submit to Joseph's orders. During the seven years of abundance the land produced plentifully. Joseph collected all the food produced in those seven years of abundance in Egypt and stored it in the cities. He stored up huge quantities of grain, just as he had suggested to Pharaoh. When the seven years of abundance in Egypt came to an end, the seven years of famine began, just as Joseph had said. There was famine in all the other lands, but in the whole land of Egypt there was food. Why? Because Joseph had been diligent in managing the food during the years of abundance. Genesis 41:56-57 (NIV) says, "*When the famine had spread over the whole country, Joseph opened all the storehouses and sold grain to the Egyptians, for the famine was severe throughout Egypt. And all the world came to Egypt to buy grain from Joseph, because the famine was severe everywhere.*" Joseph's efficient use of resources had enabled the land of Egypt to survive a severe famine. Had he not had the foresight to plan ahead, the people of Egypt would have starved to death.

Homework

The art of efficiency can wear many different hats. In the book of Genesis Joseph was efficient in the way he handled the grain during the seven years of plenty. Some people define efficiency as the ability to multi-task. For the purpose of the topic at hand, I would like for you to think of efficiency as getting the most out of your home school day. So for homework I would ask that you take a close look at your physical surroundings. Thankfully, we do not have to have a designated room in order to teach our children every day. Many of us teach around the kitchen table or on the living room couch. The location of your school is not nearly as important as the organization. Take the time to organize your most basic school supplies. Make sure that your child does not have to spend fifteen minutes searching for a pencil or notebook paper in order to complete an assignment. If your child needs a particular worksheet every Tuesday morning, make an effort the night before to have the worksheet printed and waiting for them. Designate a nice wicker basket as your library basket. All books from the library are kept in this basket until their due date. This can save loads of time turning the house upside down looking for an overdue book. Get creative. There are lots of ways to incorporate a little more efficiency into what we do.

CHAPTER 8

Exercise

Maintaining a healthy lifestyle

———⸱⸱⸱⸱———

"For physical training is of some value, but
godliness has value for all things, holding promise for
both the present life and the life to come."

1 Timothy 4:8 (NIV)

You are probably asking yourself, "What on earth does exercise have to do with educating my children at home?" or "Does every book I read have to mention the E word?" Well, relax. I am not going to lead you through a ten-step process to regain your girlish figure or chastise you for failing to put in ninety minutes of aerobic activity a minimum of four days a week. What I do want to share with you is my experience with moderate exercise and the potential benefits of maintaining some sort of consistent exercise regimen.

Before going any further, I must tell you that I was never the athletic type in school. Besides swimming on a small team as a child and running track a bit in middle school, I was never really much of an athlete. While I did not participate in many team sports, I somehow always managed to maintain my ideal weight as I evolved from middle school to high school and even into college. It was during my sophomore year of college that I first began to get serious about exercise. I had certainly done my part to support the Freshman Fifteen theory and was feeling stressed with my class workload that second year of school. I joined an on-campus aerobics class in hopes of dropping those unwanted pounds I had packed on the previous year. I was by no means overweight, but simply could not wear many of the clothes that hung in my small dorm room closet. My goal? Find a way to squeeze back into my favorite jeans that were now a size smaller than I was. My friends and I became faithful participants in that aerobics class twice a week. It was a slow start, but eventually I began to realize that I was enjoying the class and actually looking forward to it each week. Before long I noticed that I could easily slide back into those jeans in my closet, as well as other clothes that had not seen the light of day since my initial arrival at school that year. However, I quickly recognized an even greater benefit of the exercise I was getting. My mind was more at ease. I could more easily relax, and I slept like a baby when my head hit the pillow each night. Tension headaches that I had battled that semester were coming less and less often. Not only was exercise improving my physical condition, but it was bolstering my mental well-being as well. This, in my opinion, is one of the greatest benefits of maintaining an exercise routine.

Once I realized how good exercise made me feel, I committed to making it a part of my daily routine for the long haul. Do I always want to get up in the morning and jump on my exercise bike for an hour? Absolutely not. Do I look forward to walking around the block in the dead of winter with forty mile per hour winds? Of course not. However, I know that I do not have the luxury of foregoing exercise for an extended period of time. I need the mental break and the relaxation it brings. There is a huge difference in the days I exercise versus those when I do not. My tolerance is greater, my outlook is brighter, and my mind is clearer. Add the physical benefits on top of all of that, and it really is a win-win situation.

Exercise will look differently for each person. Some may enjoy a structured class at the local YMCA. Others do not like to exercise in a group and prefer to join a walking buddy for a stroll around the neighborhood several times a week. Still others long for some alone time and may choose to read while putting in their miles on a stationary bike. One is just as effective as the other when it comes to resting your mind and gaining a renewed mental energy for the task at hand. Let's face it. Home schooling can sometimes require just as much, if not more, from us mentally as it does physically. The best way I have found to rejuvenate my mind and work off some of the stress is through exercise.

For some people, morning is the best time to lace up their sneakers and pound the pavement. Others find themselves needing a break in the afternoon, and a brisk walk around the block serves to boost their enthusiasm for the high calling of home schooling. Still others enjoy a stroll with their spouse after dinner to unwind and catch up on the day. Choose whatever works best for you. One caution is to avoid exercising too close to bedtime. You may find it difficult to sleep after thirty minutes on the elliptical or an hour-long late afternoon aerobics class because your body is now energized and the adrenaline is flowing. Give your body ample time to relax before trying to catch some z's.

Paul admonishes us to present our bodies as living sacrifices

In the Old Testament God had a temple for His people; however, in the New Testament He has His people for a temple.

When we hear the word temple, we usually get a mental picture of the structure that Solomon constructed over a seven-year span of time in the Old Testament. Solomon's construction of the temple of the Lord was completed using precise measurements, specific cedar planks and blocks, and elaborate carvings. The intricate details are carefully outlined in 1 Kings chapter six. Only blocks dressed at the quarry were used, and each section of the temple was partitioned off according to a predetermined number of cubits. Special preparations were made for the inner sanctuary and the entire interior was overlaid with gold. This was a structure that was carefully crafted, not one thrown up overnight. A tremendous number of resources, including time, talent, attention, and money were devoted to the building of God's temple. The temple of the Holy Spirit, our body, should be no different.

The apostle Paul taught that we are the temple of God. First Corinthians 6:19-20 (NIV) says, "*Do you not know that your bodies are temples of the Holy Spirit, who is in you, whom you have received from God? You are not your own; you were bought at a price. Therefore, honor God with your bodies.*"

Because we have been redeemed by the death of Jesus Christ, the Holy Spirit has taken up residence on the inside of us. Under the Old Testament law the tabernacle, and later the temple, were given over entirely to God for His sacred use. They were called "holy" because they were separated and used for His purpose and glory alone.

Under the grace of the new covenant, the Christian is now called God's temple. Our bodies are sacred temples, holy unto the Lord. Paul says in Romans 12:1 (ESV), "*I appeal to you therefore, brothers, by the mercies of God, to present your bodies as a living sacrifice, holy and acceptable to God, which is your spiritual worship."* If we have learned that our body is the temple of the Holy Spirit, we will keep it undefiled and do our best to make it a suitable dwelling for God's Spirit. While there are many ways to care for and maintain our physical bodies, one of the most proven methods of maintaining a healthy body is exercise. The benefits far outweigh any excuses we could conjure up for failing to keep these temples in good working order.

Homework

I am sure you already know what your assignment is going to be. You guessed it! Find a way to work exercise into your daily (or at least weekly) routine. You do not have to spend hours and small fortunes at a local gym pumping iron and enrolling in intense spin classes. You also do not need to begin logging miles around town in an all-out effort to compete in an upcoming marathon. If those things excite you and cause you to spring out of bed each morning with a determination to do this thing in a big way, then go for it! However, for the rest of us, I am simply suggesting that we begin to incorporate some kind, any kind, of exercise into our lives. Remember, we are aiming to clear our minds, unwind, and gain a fresh perspective. All those physical benefits are just icing on the cake.

PART TWO

"I'll trade you my apple for your gummy worms."

No matter how hard we try to pack the best lunch possible, there will always be something in someone else's lunchbox that looks a little more appetizing. It happens all the time. You hear the story of the first-grader who opens his Superman lunchbox only to find a low-fat turkey sandwich on whole wheat bread spread with hummus, carrot sticks, a small box of raisins, and an apple. Next to him, a classmate sits down to a peanut butter and jelly sandwich on white bread, potato chips with dip, a package of gummy worms, and a chocolate chip granola bar. The first child leans in close and whispers, "I'll trade you my apple for your gummy worms." Pitying his friend for having to eat hummus, the classmate agrees to the trade and hands over the gummy worms.

I am currently finding myself in the throes of such a trade-off. You see, I have been diligent to pack the right lunch. I have made every attempt to "feed" my kids what I consider to be a healthy diet of home school curricula, social etiquette, and spiritual discipline. For the last eleven years I have devoted myself to educating my kids at home. I do not regret a single day of it. I would not trade this time with my kids for anything on earth. Have my efforts been perfect? Absolutely not. Do I find myself taking three steps forward and one step back along this journey? Daily. However, I truly believe that home schooling is the closest we can operate to the Biblical model of education presented in the Bible. I have made my share of mistakes along the way, but this journey is one of the most rewarding experiences of my life, and I am most grateful for it.

With that said, we are currently considering sending our oldest daughter to private school next year. In a way, it is like trading our juicy red apple for a package of sugar-laden gummy worms. Both may serve as dessert, but the apple is actually a better choice for our bodies. Home school and private school both serve to educate our children, but it is my belief that home school is a better choice. If that is really the case, then why am I considering private school over home school for my daughter? That is a great question and is one I am working through myself little by little. The only thing I know for sure is that it is a most difficult decision. I began home schooling my daughter when she was four years old. I wanted to get a good feel for what this whole home school experience was like, so we completed a full-year K4 program that year. She has been home ever since. This year, she is completing her freshman year and does the majority of her work, except for the dissections, independently. She is a good student and plans to attend college after graduation to study pediatric nursing.

However, there are not many opportunities for home schoolers in our area. My daughter loves to sing, but there is not a home school choral group or choir to get involved with in our area. She also enjoys running and would love to join a school team. However, laws in our state do not allow a home school student to participate in school sports. She plans to enter a field that will require a good foundation in science. While we are successfully completing biology at home this year, it has not been easy. The dining room table doubles as biology lab. Next year she will take chemistry, and those labs get even more technical and involved. The very last thing I want to do is short-change her in any way, but in some ways I can see that happening. I know many home school parents opt out during their child's high school years because they feel inadequate or incapable of teaching the more advanced subjects. I do not feel that we are considering private school just because my daughter is an upcoming sophomore. It has much less to do with her grade in school and much more to do with a change in our hearts. We feel that we have taken her as far as we are supposed to take her, and God is asking us to consider a change for next year.

As I look back over all the reasons why we chose to home school in the first place, I am finding that it is just as important to know when it is time to send our children to school. For some parents, that may mean fourth grade. For others, God may call them to home school their children until middle school or until they reach high school. Still others may see their children graduate from home school. The important thing is to know when the time is right for your family.

I have wrestled with this decision for months now and have grown weary in the process. I think deep down I know God is calling me to do this, but I simply am not ready for my eldest to detour from this familiar journey we have taken together. As I was praying about this decision one day, God showed me a passage of Scripture in Nehemiah that gave me a path forward. After reading about Nehemiah earlier in this book, you know that he was leading a charge to rebuild the fractured walls of Jerusalem. This was no easy task. Certain individuals attempted to halt the work by continually ridiculing and threatening the workers. Eventually the workers grew tired, both physically and emotionally. Nehemiah 4:10-12 (NIV) says, *"Meanwhile, the people in Judah said, 'The strength of the laborers is giving out, and there is so much rubble that we cannot rebuild the wall.' Also our enemies said, 'Before they know it or see us, we will be right there among them and will kill them and put an end to the work.' Then the Jews who lived near them came and told us ten times over, 'Wherever you turn, they will attack us.'"*

Verses thirteen and fourteen describe how Nehemiah responded. *"Therefore I stationed some of the people behind the lowest points of the wall at the exposed places, posting them by families, with their swords, spears and bows. After I looked things over, I stood up and said to the nobles, the officials and the rest of the people, 'Don't be afraid of them. Remember the Lord, who is great and awesome, and fight for your families, your sons and your daughters, your wives and your homes.'"* God showed me that verse ten was a picture of me. My strength was giving out and I was growing exceedingly weary. Verse eleven was symbolic of my fears. The verse implies that the enemy will put an end to all the hard work. That is one of my greatest fears. We have invested eleven years of our lives into home schooling, and I fear that private school could potentially unravel all of our efforts. However, God had me camp on verse fourteen. It says, *"Don't be afraid of them. Remember the Lord, who is great and awesome, and fight for your families, your sons and your daughters, your wives and your homes.*" In other words, my work is far from over. If my daughter ends up attending school outside our home, my work only intensifies. My job is to fight for my daughter. How do I do that? On my knees. I have already begun to pray God's protection over her. I pray that her dependence on Him would be greater than ever. No, everything we have worked so hard to accomplish at home does not have to be lost when she enters school. She is just being given an opportunity to put into practice all she has learned.

I share this with you to encourage you to pack the best lunch you can possibly pack. Be sure to pack a variety of fresh fruits and vegetables and incorporate something from each of the four basic food groups. However, always realize that a time may come when you are asked to trade your apple for someone else's gummy bears. When and if that time comes, approach your decision carefully knowing that He who began a good work will complete it.